BADHULI

POEMS

BY

Dr. ALOK KUMAR RAY

BOOK PRESS

BHARAT INTERNATIONAL BOOK PRESS

SURYA SEN STREET, KOLKATA-95, BERHAMPORE, W.B

BADHULI

Dr. Alok Kumar Ray

Published by : Bharat International Book Press

Published on : 1st May, 2026

Distributed by: Bi Book Press & amazon.com

ISBN No : 978-93-5812-728-7

Page count : 128

Edition : First

Cover by: Dr. Ratan Ghosh, Director, **BI BOOK PRESS**

SURYA SEN STREET, KOLKATA-95,

Berhampore, Pin 742103

Contact no of Publisher: **7001127572**.

Email:bibookpresspublication@gmail.com

E-mail Author- alokray1966@gmail.com

Kindle EBook INR. 150/$8

Paperback INR 300/ $15

Hardbound INR 399/$22

Legal terms and conditions

Acknowledgement

I express my gratitude to the publisher for decorating 'Badhuli' with his own thoughts, for providing the rationale by own efforts and for embracing it at his own risks. Along with I am immensely indebted to sir. Williamsji Maveli for inking a Foreword for this poetry anthology,'Badhuli'.

Dr. Alok Kumar Ray

Dedication

I am now free from answerability by entrusting 'Badhuli' to my own sibling, 'Babu'.

Some word petals relating to 'Badhuli'......

Painting the palms or feet with 'Badhuli' (Balsams) is not only a manifestation of beauty and thirst for the flowers by girls and women but also another captivating appeal of the eternal attraction for feminine traits. This effort of a girl or a woman to verbalize her expression in public under the guise of traditional knowledge and artistic skill always confesses engagingly the essence of our prevalent social system. In which the best elegance standing at the forefront utters. In a compassionate time of the seasonal cycle-based system, Badhuli smiles in the garden. Out of the many varieties of red, pink, velvet, white etc., red Badhuli is everyone's favorite and is the perfect tool for decorating hands and feet. While on the tree red Badhuli portrays the intoxicating nature of red lips. The vague message of the primitive hypnosis it spreads in the air. After spending a few days on the tree, the petals of the colorful flower fall one by one. Putting a pause on the way of the flying mind, it explains the dignity of the soil. It succumbs to the needs of the time so much vulnerable. Be it the heart of a woman or a girl, as there is no hope for a little understanding and too much ignorance permeates, there due to deepening depth instead of propelling the boat by an oar, rowing remains as the only option. Even the moon in such a case is lost in the waves of the mind, as it fails to grasp the law that prevails. However the color of the Badhuli sits as before capturing a secluded place in the mind of women or girls. Badhuli leaves its home, becomes homeless, daughter will become, so also a woman. Badhuli 's petals fall down one after another, the daughter also and so also a woman. They are champions in the field of falling down, the epitome of negligence. Badhuli falls on the ground, feels deserted, the daughter meets the same fate and so also a woman as time passes. Throughout the year, Badhuli does not stay, her transformation continues unabatedly. The girl does not remain a daughter for all the times, she becomes a bride, a woman, a mother, and widow. The daughter or woman, in tune with the Badhuli bites herself at every moment even without any provocation. Affected by her own poison she falls down adhering to own fate. She somehow takes care of herself, and even after being thrown on the soil, she thinks it is better to reside inside the earth, become the scapegoat like Sita but not raising any sorts of protests that challenge the existing stereotypes. Both the chronological and virtual panoramic ideas linked to Badhuli though speak less but showcase an ambience where everything remaining below the ashes establish their presence in the ephemeral shape of dust and smoke.

Dr. Alok Kumar Ray

FOREWORD

The human condition is a complex, multifaceted entity, encompassing the depths of human emotion, the struggles of existence, and the quest for meaning. Dr. Alok Kumar Ray's collection of poems delves into the intricacies of human experience, exploring themes of self-discovery, societal chaos, love, and awakening.

The poems in this collection are a reflection of the human condition, with all its contradictions and paradoxes. They grapple with existential questions, societal critiques, and the search for meaning in a world full of contradictions. The poet's introspection reveals a life of monotony, a cycle of wanting more; yet, this awareness sparks a desire to break free.

The "monkey mind", driven by greed and instinct, is a potent metaphor for the human struggle. The poet's comparison of themselves to a monkey, jumping from one thing to another, captures the essence of this struggle. The poems invite the reader to reflect on their own existence, to question their desires, and to seek a deeper understanding of themselves.

The sky, a symbol of shared humanity, is partitioned by "sweet wills" and "tainted beliefs". The poems critique divisive ideologies, urging a return to unity. The result of this division is chaos, a world infected by "the virus of utter chaos". The poems call for recognition of our shared humanity, a call to transcend the boundaries that divide us.

The poems describe love as "sacred and clinically driven", a force that endures despite adversity. It's the "language of an infant", soothing and pure. This love isn't about possession but connection — a means to transcend pettiness. The poems call for awakening to the world's suffering. "Let's wake up for a Bumper investment in unison" — the urgency is palpable.

True change requires shedding apathy, seeing the "unseen, uncut screenings" around us. The poems invite the reader to wake up, to recognize the suffering, and to act.

Dr. Ray's poetry is a powerful exploration of the human condition, tackling issues like social justice, technology's impact on relationships, and mental health. His use of diverse voices and styles conveys the complexity of human emotions, from love to trauma. The collection also explores the symbolism of 'Badhuli' (Balsams), a flower that represents the beauty and fragility of life.

The poet reflects on the societal constraints that shape the lives of women, and the importance of recognizing and challenging these norms. Through this collection, Dr. Alok Kumar Ray offers a profound and thought-provoking exploration of the human condition, inviting readers to reflect on their own existence and the world around them.

In the poet's own words, "Badhuli" is a poetic expression of eternal thoughts and habitual but cross-cultural overtones like life and livelihood, love and passion, both earthly and heavenly joys and sorrows.

Dr. Ray's poetry is a testament to the enduring power of poetry to capture the human experience, and this collection is a must-read for anyone seeking to understand the complexities of human existence.

WILLIAMSJI MAVELI

An eminent Author, Editor and, Philosopher

CONTENTS

BADHULI

POEMS

Am I a monkey?

When I introspect myself in serendipity;
Willingly start an inward journey
To compute 'how far I have gone',
whether kissed the pinnacle of success,
Set new and alluring standards for the value-starved posterity?
Or which key tips I have overlooked,
by design have tried to conceal facts and figures!
Indeed I discern no new things;
not an islet where spring reigns for aeons,
No new ideas whatsoever could I be able to delineate!
The same thing,
Hustle and bustle of mundane life;
animalistic instinct of greediness to acquire more,
Enjoying sound asleep while nightmare hovers around,
Engrossing in fright for losing life, comfort zone, kith and kin,
Drenched in sensual pleasure while overlooking prescriptions,

All these findings reminded me that I am a monkey.
Jumps from one rooftop to another,
discharges excreta and urine while eating,
Ravages much more than requisite to meet both ends,
Reasonably astounding!

The Sky

They wanted to split up and dole out the sky among themselves
As per their sweet wills, the values which suit them the most,
The philosophies which they worship with open eyes
Albeit the rich and affable history of human race.

And consciously unaware of drenched eye lids of the sky,
Its immenseness that houses even the vacuum
They didn't pay any heed to a clarion call coming from within
To respect the status quo that exemplified as glorious.

The wind was murmuring song of the war in full swing;
While tainted beliefs trying to get safe passage at any cost,

The whole ambience was infected by the virus of utter chaos,
And the news of falling sky had made sane minds dubious.

People were wearing with ease myriads of colourful glasses;
With them they were trying to anyhow typify the sky,
Giving it name of diverse types notwithstanding own silliness,
Ignoring its all-pervasive and limitless, utmost expanse.

They were trying to paint its surface with hues of divide and rule;
Even someone was attempting to erase its azure colour in haste.
Although the sky was still savouring all types of prayers and hymns
Its neutrality has become a bone of contention surpassing all reasons.

Whether the sky was gloomy or transparent or cloudy,
All were in tight lips to answer for reasons mysterious and hazy.
Markets were flooding with even secondhand goggles
The guts to assess judiciously was losing its potency in this mess.

Platonic Love

Love is not something that can be forsaken
It's sacred and clinically driven
For two souls to enjoy the blissful grace
Of the Almighty in a serene ambience

Like morning hymn love is subtle
It can endure Himalayan pressure but can't brittle
It's like the language of an infant very soothing
Lovelorn souls resist pitfalls in love making

Its foundation is strong to counter adulterous pilferage
There is no question of any types of sacrilege
It's adorned by selflessness crown
Love birds save each other from falling down

Though Platonic Love seems misnomer to some
The very idea cherishes lofty sense to overcome
Bitterness among two loveable souls ready to plunge
Into ocean of long lasting love to which both belong

Awakening

From deep slumber let's wake up for a
Bumper investment in unison
Open up your eyes to see the unseen, uncut
Screenings surrounded.
How age old values, traditions are
Crumbling fast
Like house of cards unhindered and undiagnosed.
Listen to the gossips of people in
Camouflage, feel hues and cries still unnoticed,
Their agony, misfortunes and sufferings are aired in volume
Which only need a spark to ignite their
Lethargic inner being,
Just a step ahead, a leap forward will bring a new dawn.
At the end of the tunnel there will be light
Radiating brightness
At one go awaken the entire
Circumambience kept in dormant, infected
By misgivings in full swing!

Phulrijharan

On the back keeping large stretches of greenery
Initiating a game of shadow and light here and there,
everywhere
At an orderly yard offering cooled and silent ambience
On the other side of the serpentine, blackish road
Below the competition between shrubs and vines
 to touch sunlight
Near harsh, distasteful sounds of wild animals
Amidst high -pitched,
monotonous chirping of unknown birds
Near the transit point of journey loving aboriginals'
who keep the environment in their pockets
Frank and the fresh environment's heart touching,

attracting magic

Word knitting natural environment

under the authority of

hills, springs, jungle, local people, flora and fauna

Flowery dripping of water by Phulrijharan,

mesmerizes mind, mingles the heart with peace.

Note: ***Phulrijharan is a waterfall***

situated in Kalahandi district of Odisha, India

Daughter

Altering frequently stature

With time, with situation, with surroundings

Has taken the vow for an amicable defrayal

Always skilled to put together

Keeps the three fold oath of fusion

A simple, tall but slim, emotion driven girl

Seeks for moon in the broad day light sky.

Without grasping the basics of mathematical calculations

Possibly she finally put question mark on remainder

Possibly she befalls glad by smearing the division with an addition

She is a fierce adversary of deletion, impediment

For her, burgeoning of glee is a huge burden

Accounting of mathematics in her vocabulary
Only is a hopeless error.

She values beauty, adores also
Her mind is obsessed with opulence, sure
For her, formation, situation, rhythms are only social shock
Of renunciation she is the epitome, unusual
Whole expression of love and longing is she, boundless
Facsimile of tolerance is she,
Of the tradition of admiration, she is the golden counterpart.

Daughter

After the aroma of a rapport
That is not being shaken
That is beyond the clutches of hugging
That is afar the capacity of an eye to grab
Spreads anonymous wings,
With the backing of a conspirator cloud, the rain
Clapping its hands created a fake river.
Drawing the line of partition while the river was flowing
Water bubbles burst with laughter.
Waves in the form of braids
Stretched from this shore to that shore.
Instead of causing landslips
They turn into an overpass that touched both shores.
Getting the ford, getting the shelter, bonding grew up.

After the wrath of the unseasonable rain caved in

After the vanishing of the bigoted river

The intricacy of rowing the boat

Since long is being mortgaged sans notice.

There is no dispute that could insist overpowering

Not a viable trace is visible now.

The flat chest of that died river now adorns

Flowers and fruits in plenty, fortune and affection

Where sings the song of delight and contentment,

The time of a daughter, defiant and wild.

Girl

The peril that surfaces if one falls asleep consciously
In the arms of darkness in night,
In a small space within that ambience,
When the cost of breathing enhances,
And beginning of conspiracy to scold the wind opens up
Among many, one emerges
She sits serenely holding the sound of silence
She says nothing,
But becoming the source of many things for everyone
She just beholds.

As the night grows older,
She gathers darkness through her long veil
Not throwing out makes it her eyes' collyrium
Keeps it hiding within her unsmooth thick hair?
Before the trust is lost being despicable
Making it morning star pitches in the chest of the night.
Swimming in the fog fills the breathing with consolation
Rubbing feet in morning dews
In welcoming stance pleases one and all.

Baby's time to get up from the soil

Rubbing and rubbing your tender body,
Your first crawling
First, first, relying on the broken and stammering words
The intimate call of "Daddy" and "Mummy"
I remember my daughter, as the main event of yesterday
Today, like the memory on the front page of the newspaper,
With a photo in bold letters is being flash upon
Carbon copy, unadulterated.

Every day, though I became partially successful in untimely removing your finger from your mouth

I saw inside that opening of mouth
Near the thin layer of artistic and reddish cave
The joy of childish agility, free from temptation.

Behind the anxiety of being kept in arm-pit,
The desire to gather safety,
The fashion to sleep keeping your head on my shoulder,
The irresistible intention,
Again the blooming smile that emanating from your face
when you were offered gifts ,
I reminisce it like yesterday, fondly remembering.

Your round and cute face,
Being full of the snot coming out of your running nose,
Devastated in the flood of tears,
Inundation of your flower garden of the chin
Now reminiscing, as if it were
An emotional scene from some social drama.

Amidst the daily
routinely tricks of eating and drinking
The unforgettable feeling of feeding you
Being a star twinkling in my mind's sky,
I still soak in that faint light,

Day or night, every moment.

My daughter, the precious moments
of your awakening from the soil
Do not allow me to sleep
Now, how long will I sit idly being lethargic?

Blurred Destination

I had waited for a candle light dinner with you
But while searching your whereabouts on the courtyard
I felt liquid larva like expectations oozing out from my heart
Air was filled with alluring temptations
Even in that snowy evening hour
I felt the warmth of the bygone memories.

To someone whom I love more than me,
To something which I had been longing for a long time,
To someplace quite ideal for two lovelorn souls
to carry forward sensual gossips
To somewhere touching
fathomless feelings albeit fazing innocence
My being collided with expectations alluring
against the reality, ever encompassing.

The car in which once we had heard
solitude speaking aloud

The pottery like initial interactions was very easier to mould
The silent moments that succumbed to our whispers,
That plague drawn cleavages between our prancing breaths
From where I used to gather tiny but amusing solace pieces
Found I, bereft of any needs and deeds to overcome the crisis.

I could overlook lewd remarks by the bystanders
'Come and wrap me in placidity, find tranquility
while being infused in astounding,
inflammable and ravenous labyrinthine chasm
While the world was enveloped
by clouds of jealousy
Right beneath our impeccable cozy heart
love bud was blooming fast, but
Heavy hearts are susceptible indeed!

True Humanist

If someone expresses his sorrows
Writes in vivid languages of pain
Showcases the cause of his misery
through protests on the streets

Raise voice and demonstrate in the public against
involuntary attacks, violence, hatred, barbarity, etc.
on his own race, religion, belief, tradition,
language, and culture, etc.
In a democratic, peaceful, harmonious,
and law abiding way
Like a drowning person taking refuge
by catching at a straw mat,

He protests, protests, shouts slogans against the government
To protect himself, his family, and mundane property, etc.

He raises his voice for the comfortable and safe journey

of his relatives and friends perching in the same boat

If the media seeking news agency
Reports this self-inflicted assault

If persons perform their duty by being saddened,
giving space ,
If many deceived, persecuted,
marginalized and trampled human groups like him,
Raise their hands in cooperation,
become equally sad, perform peaceful protests,
Narrate negatively and harshly criticize the
powerful government and administration,
Will these individuals be criticized?
for being victims of narrow-mindedness
in pursuance of protecting humanity?

The countless people who agree with the individual,
who keep the flame of cooperation burning,
Will those few people who are trapped in the web of

so-called narrow-mindedness
be especially condemned?

By defining the definition of humanity
according to their own wishes,
Keeping own status, reputation, own interests,
own so-called future under the safe umbrella,
How can anyone ever be a true humanist?

Moon gathering Girl

Half-moon in the mid night
Moon gathering girl's mind doesn't obey, gets it
She needs a full moon of the full moon day,
bright moon of the autumn sky
Who appears during twilight hours?
Who hides behind the shadow of coconut tree leaves
Who is the storehouse of cool light?
Who sees her face in pond's transparent water?
Who caters Lilly the fire of longing?
Unique joy, unforgettable
Who on the white paper of a virgin's mind?
Depicts the fountain of colors sans any obstacles
Who when grows from the second lunar day
to attain youth at the full moon , simply smiles
Who, at the eve of Kumar Purnima
renders a touch of love 's chalk
in the heart of a million young women
Who sometimes plays hide and seek
with wind surviving within the gap of clouds
Who by bringing tide in seas and rivers?

multiplies the fame of the world .
Moon gathering girl needs serene moon,
Sans dust moving cool light.
One day, thinking that she would hug the moon,
On the pond she spread her saree
One day to grab the moon,
convincing the clouds became, she mate lying
One day seeing the moon on the tenth day
of the lunar fortnight morning
she fainted
One day, depicting the moon in her mathematics notebook,
she became the butt of jokes
One day while with friends, talking about moon,
she wore the ornaments of shame.
One day, on a rainy night,
she cried restlessly without seeing the moon.
The absence of the moon on the new moon day each time
caused for her great pain
Whether it is Ketugrasa or Rahugrasa lunar eclipse,
she suffered enunciated widowhood

Moon gathering girl observed in twelve months thirteen Osha,
had not touched food or water.
The very day that girl set foot in the city,
Moon under the mask of unmarried girl hid the face
The lights of the city instead of teasing her
offered flowers and sandalwood paste.
The flawless moon of the full moon day was lost
Forgot the address of the Moon, moon gathering girl.

Daughter

The patriarchal adultery in tune with
alternation of lineage ,name, village, address and family
Strengthened by the potency of society, unyielding assortment
Famous by the name of tradition, renowned customs
There emerges again religious constraints, mortal
The temporal therapy at the time of daughter's departure
As worldly rule dominates, the earth and the infinite seem constrained.

All the troubles begin from the womb
If the daughter -fetus grows in the mother's womb
In food, clothing, sleep and lifestyle deficiency rules
In the family system, termination appears
Innocent mother churns within, opts silent crying
Keeping a stone on the chest, bears countless pains
Like a leaf in the stream, her price is negligible.

The girl's food, clothing, attire, transportation
Education, initiation, conversation and upbringing
Everywhere is seen literally compliance with the special rules
When her age succumbs to the fire of youth
Thousands of day dreams may sprout in the mind of men
Depicted as an object of consumption, gets no care at all
Like a waste product, her present and after life is of no importance.

The daughter is the confluence of creator, creation, and pleasure
Give her honor, respect, and a high position
Learn from her love, compassion, renunciation, and tolerance
She is the eternal spring of humanity, be like her
She guides social current as a mother, sister, and daughter-in-law
She sets the clue for our age -old journey of life
Get the rudiments of a value-based society from her.

Daughter

With patience repaired I many of her broken toys since she was a child,
And in return, I have been captivated
By the cloudy weather of fulfillment rising from her face.

During play, while playing with her friends,
Behind the shadow of the bickering, I have felt
The sweetness of her judgment tactics
Her own pledge existed between winning and losing.

The blood clot that oozing out of a torn knee or elbow
Before being coagulated
I have seen the pale flame of restlessness,
Its growing twigs at the door end of culmination.

Even after skipping food and drinking,
Her urge to finish school tasks
Before her Himalayan like obstinacy
how powerless was mother's endearment

l have seen along passion being still and stable
Standing in a waiting posture.

To grow, for growth pullulating
Fight, for fight consecration,
To win, for winning invocation
In the fealty sacred fire oblation of grit
Has crafted for her now, I know
Alluring sensation of the dreamy mustard field.

Proficiency and excellence
After taking feet off the labour room of diligence
I am only a spellbound spectator now.

Sometimes the smile of the sugarcane field engulfs my face
Sometimes in my eyes there is the language of honeyed estuary
Sometimes in my mouth there is full of praise
For the sky bound kite .

Daughter

Like an arrow falling from a bow

Like words slipped out of mouth

The girl is gone, that's it

Jumping over ancestral home of many generations.

She is as non -returning as Rukuna Chariot

As preternatural as a past memory

As unique as a dream of yesterday

She is as invisible as Water absorbed by the soil.

When stretches out hands towards her

The sun, moon, and stars fall from the sky

If run after her to chase

Sinks the ground, creating a reservoir.

She has taken within her cupped hands

blessings from parental home
Socked with tears,
haunting memories and irreversible stare
The pleasant experiences depicted
by bright red dye on the soles of her feet
Scorched permission in the shade of her veil.

Learning to weave the world's spider net
She by tucking in the sarees corner in her waist
Will get right her mother-in-law's house
by straightening her spine
Will unite the broken earthen horse
Overpowered by belongingness
Will offer aromatic bouquets of flowers.

Daughter

With a little lighted laughter and a bit of panicking tears
She has gone far away, to her mother-in-law's house
The leaves of time have turned in the meantime
The definition of messiness has revamped slightly
The intensity of responsibility has been flooded
The seduction of duty has increased the pulsation.

Between going and coming, one huge
Desire of separation stiffens
A dreadful ghost appears in the chest
In thought many waves rise and fall to touch
the shore of possibility , extinguish without touching
The crow flaps its wings with gratification after gobbling.

With a little sweetness in thinking and a dash of salty anger
The girl will return to her father's house

The wind of euphoric gentle smile will blow continuously
At the door of the house, the festive season will knock
The thrilling archway will shine all around
The teary eyes will remain awake all night.

Place of composition: Cuttack
Odia version published in the Apurba, 2024

The Girl

Wearing the change prone pseudonym of time,
Trying to prove oneself as progressive
Drawing a dynamic full stop
Before the explosion of the deep argument of gender discrimination
You all the custodians of the society
After washing your face seven times in the holy Ganges
Look at yourself in the mirror of truth
And weigh yourself, your existence, the call of time,
the seven custodians of directions
Check out through the weigh machine of reality
The genealogy of gap within social authority
Throwing afar the pride of self interest
And hug the unused possibilities of the community.

Apart from the divinely created natural system,
By taking oaths, by creating a cycle of social stability,

Easily erecting circular trap of firmness
Basing on the imaginary line of law man-made
By easily diverting the flow of time
By stifling the throat of progress,
You, all high profile social care takers
Throw away your unauthorized ego, wounded vanity,
By undoing your manliness
By removing the cataract from your own eyes, and watch gazingly
How change leaving fatigue is rushing to create a new world,
City of Yakshas
Realize that the new arrangement is designed for you
An evenly decorated playground
bereft of son and daughter discrimination.

Moon in the City

It is natural to lose the moon in the city
Like losing wallet without knowing it
Or loosing self-control due to alcohol intoxication.

In that way, getting lost in the city
And accumulating fun by losing something is distinct.
When night falls, many things disappear in the city
In the light of day, many things
Becoming pain bang the head in the outskirts.

The blood of the city is always fresh
In it, comforts, conveniences
The inestimable accumulated capital of glamour are washed away.

There is no such thing as the sky of the city
Nor is there the scented smell of the earth
Only that the wind runs from one end to the other
Nor is there the coolness nor the inebriating power of the sandalwood forest.

This time, however, the city is flooded with
the light of the moon
Remaining within the mouth of earthquake
After all the lights of the city have gone out,
To inspect the cries of the distressed people,
The rotten odour milieu
The moon is roaming around at night,
Holding the dimly lit torch of the moon light in its hand.

Even during the day, the moon is visible
In the brain of newspapers
In the eyes of the television
In the speeches of the leaders and their colleagues,
In the company of the relief agencies,
In toto at the sacred spot of distressed people's heartfelt eyes.

Moon Garden

You want to see its reflection in the pond,
hoping not to be caught in the moon garden

But I wait for season after season,

and when autumn comes,

I see the moon in the clear retina of your eyes

The shimmering eye balls of yours,

overwhelmed by the sweet pain of

not being able to hold back tears,

dies in shame.

Please say, why your face becomes splendid
when you bathe in the light of the moon?

I am not a party to it, even not attached,

what is the use of a ripe wood apple for the crow ?

Like your lips, wherever the moon yawns,

I see there the acceptance of a

Star-studded bizarre lover.

I am a student in the first grade of love,

for whom the judgment is shrill between

what is usable and unusable, sin and virtue,

worthy of reverence and despicable.

Yes, I am indiscreet,

my mind and body are tied to the scales of pleasure.

Staying on the other side of that parenthesis,
like you many heroines ,
not interested in going inside the garden of the moon,
meet me in search of the pond.
You know, I dislike meeting with anyone without offerings,
just as when the eastern wind blows ,
sounds of the whistle becomes audible.
Leave that ' talk, let's go to the garden of the moon together,
even if only once,
eat all the forbidden fruits,
fill up fragrance in stinking flowers,
hold the moon in the palm lifted from the sky,
You will say the moon is cursed,
from full moon to new moon it changes shape
I will say the moon is afflicted,
many people like you do not understand
their own kins and believe in reflections.

(The original Odia poem written by the poet was published in the foreign web magazine ' Dylan day ', Raging Moon-Dylan Thomas,2024)

Paranani

You said that with a wink of an eye,
the cloud will grow here and there, everywhere
I said Paranani held tightly the cloud yesterday
near the fence brazenly.

You said that this cloud is a wanton, malevolent
, not a black cloud at all
I said that if there were backings
the cloud would blow whistle notwithstanding
weeds.

You said that even without blowing whistle
cloud is grown early, in the morning, at all times
I said that without thinking about the result, the
cloud
Is hooked on the mountain tops untimely.
You said that the water cannot flow
from high to low, very low sans the rooftop
I said that from below, when I saw , not the cloud
but
I like the sky so much.
Speaking like the sky, you said,

don't go so far from the context
I said, the distant mountain looks beautiful
if it cuddles the clouds without napping.
What is the lap, again with an oblique glance you asked me
with questioning eyes, doubting me
I put my head on your lap to gain patience
and awkwardly acted as accurately as I could.
Then, without saying anything,
you bowed your head and planted a kiss
on my forehead quickly
On the other side, till the cloud ripened and fell,
Paranani eloped away very quickly.

Loveable Daughter

My loveable daughter asked me once
To bring her the buoy
Meant in general for angling.

I shook my head to refuse
Disbursing smile like a cunning politician,
Just like the Monalisha.

She said, "Oh. Shit
you are not that good!"
As a father, you ferry people
From one bank to another in a boat every day,
Rowing in a fashion that
the water looks like tearing apart,
And your head's sweating reflects on it,
And you are moving the boat forward
cutting the current ,
And all your knots are loosening,
Your face looks clear.

Not to answer
Only adding sugar to the talking
Keeping tongue amidst teeth
Sans any intention to taste the sweetness, juice
Told me in a very low voice containing tough words -
Fishes are now very in disciplined and clever
No need for a buoy now
Come, Come dear spread the veil of the saree
Me holding the other side
As I used to hold you while reading books
Keep the saree tightly
Till the water becomes a slight reddish
We two both like this
Will go on talking,
upon our heads will reside shadowing light .

A story box for my daughter

All the afternoon time, the whole evening
Used to open on every holiday
the story box
From that small to big, too many stories
Jumping like fish from a overcrowded pond
Taking refuge in my mouth, Depending on my attitude
Only for you my daughter,
With the intention of drawing a rainbow
In your mind's sky.

Too many profound but imaginary stories
Again from the Puranas
to the autobiographies of great men
The endless stream of simple words,
dazzling with traditions
Which steeped in one after another holding hands,
To depict in your mind a dotted palace of dreams.

As time passes away, it over turns

But we used to walk in another world,
One is the orator and the other is the listener
In this short period of emotional exchange
One person's words pouring from the mouth
make another happy,
And used to test then you
the limits of my concentration .

Sometimes, the child of my boredom
holds a plate of my sorrow
And begs for a temporary break
In the midst of my begging,
you used to smile a little or cry incessantly
Again story emerges to console you
Silence is driven away
Captures the scene another wet period of stories.

Now in quite solitude sometimes reminiscing
In the body of the story
Ignition of fire may not be like before
The circle of smoke may not paint
Terrified eyes of ghosts
You , me and our story box of those days are now prisoned

Inside a cosy chamber made up of gold
Placed inside one silver chest under the deep water
No one has that gut to speak in favour of those days of ours.

Daughter

The trust you had established in front of me,
The trust you had built in my mind,
On the backdrop of asking to get the moon on your palms
The eye catching highest image of faithfulness
that you had built in your mind ' canvas
Remains in my mind, my daughter, my only one.

Varieties of dolls that you wanted the most
Mouth watering eateries
That I couldn't afford
Corresponding sensitivity, anger, rage, and tears of yours
All of which I will always remember, remain with me for ever.

Your eagerness to study,
Your desire to participate in the games and to win,
Remember I one by one
Your memories seem to flash upon before my eyes like a movie,

Occupy my whole mind as a memory, very romantic.

During the higher educational stage
That is full of so many unsung, unknown deeds,
An endless cycle of breaking and joining,
An eternal process of bending and straightening,
Which makes my mind feel like yesterday,
Revealing the reason for existence.

There is a difference between seeing the moon in the sky and
Seeing its reflection on the pond, my daughter
Putting lotus stems like fear aside will gather the moon
Even if not able to catch the moon,
But not forget to stretch hands towards the moon.

Daughter

Getting wet in water causes cold
The day knew you,
From that day, embracing the rain
In wet feet, you go on with the flow.

Putting hands in fire causes burning
The day knew you,
From that day, tucking the fire into the waist,
You are laughing and making everyone laugh.

Keeping feet on the moss invites feet slipping
The day knew you,
From that day, without holding back emotions
Expounding to us the meaning of liberation.

In curbing the forbidden agility of the young age
Of the youth nurturing eye sprinkler
That your delicate body can soak,
endure the vow of four months (rainy season)
In the mountain hole, you can observe a fire festival
In deleting coats of the moss from the stone

You can give life to it by the foot touch
Even if no one knows, I know
I have tested it through the touch stone of fatherhood
On the foundation of doctrine
I have heard the sound of the conch shell
of all these being established.

Odia version published in the magazine 'Jugashri Jugnari', 2024
English transcription published in Venus in Scorpio Poetry Blog
25th April,2026

Daughter's Birth Time

On the other side of the valley of gender discrimination
Where the market of values was gathering
In the hairdo of the dry river that flowed by
When you were born as a flower
In the dry river, the hypnotic sound
of the rippling ,brimming water flow heard
That day, there were twinkling stars all around the sky
Playing with the darkness game of hide and seek
Time sans running away craving to sit down
To take a break sitting on the verandah
ornamented with rice pasted folk art
To hold the hand of potency while smiling a little.

In the silent phase of night, a supernatural uproar
Heard from the river side city induced with malice
That night was not like the veiling stingy beloved
Or like sweet sixteen hankering after the heap of optimisms
Reigning in the city like a skeleton

A rashing blurred dot of moon light.

In this moment of the earthly and supernatural juncture
You caressed the ground, found there nectar like mother's breast
Saw the earth not being skeptical, unperturbed
Fearing the wreckage, all the so-called theological reforms
Remained busy probing for social safeguards of their own
Occurrence of turning off the pages of the traditional book
Still going on being the eternal journey of the process.

Will surely you grasp this issue
Will never be the target of an unchosen sacred fire
By being called a girl, like clarified butter
Needs there a line of dignity to link between tough and nodding.

Odia version published in the Silashri, 2024
English transcription published in Venus in Scorpio Poetry Blog, 25th April, 2026

The Girl

Wild fire engulfs the Sal forest every year
The bloodied hands clap
The bare bodies look jet -black
The house of the leaping greenery ruins
There boiling heat blooms in awakening shades
The passion linked to the moonlit forest shos away.

Inside these, a girl seeks for her father
When she cries out, the echo answers
She stretches her eyes miles and miles
Heat of the fire obliges her body to feel lightheadedness.

The veins in her legs speak out every thing
Of woes, tender pride, despair and dignity
Her hands rummages through here and there
Accumulated effort of love, devotion, compassion and kindness.

Finds she her father, again father mingles away in the air
The daughter weeps profusely, her lips suck tears
Being piqued she sits under the burnt tree

Draws her father's image on the ground with charcoal
Converse with her father, she kisses him on the cheek
Two drops of tears flow from her eyes
One drop sings the virtues of adolescence
And the other drop vows of the youth.

The poem was composed at: Cuttack

(Originally written by the poet in Odia and published in the 'Saurabh' 2024.)

Fatherhood

Unconditional relationship
After getting the whereabouts of a flowery bed
Where will the flood of tears come?
To make scars on the eyelids of dreams
The endless flood of misfortune?

In the grand gathering of joys
Beholding the celebration of the lamps of possibilities
Will fatherhood draw a complete full stop?
In the fear of the unseen ritual of relationship
Holding the unforgettable warmth of the pen?

The father who walked holding hands
Embraced when stumbled
Now in Margashira, the fatherhood
After watching the dance of the ripen paddy head -buds
Drawing a Jhoti in the heart's yard!

Midst the promotion of relationships,

The father's heart is now enjoying

Amongst millions of happy dreams

The new morning brings in joyous feelings

The excitement is a brand new elevated comfort.

Nature's Ripples

Vernal springtime preparing its last rites stepping up the right leg
Quickly swallowing colours myriad in the rest peg
This scorching midsummer piercing like pincer so pathetic
Only the lone bee while kissing flowers singing a song optimistic

Flowers visible in this sultry humid ambit serve the scenic beauty
Accept or not the nature covertly doing its rightful duty
In this seasonal juncture ask for anything vibrant except pity
Singing of the cuckoo inside the mango grove seems bounty

New foliage in boughs decor trees in superb emerald
Right time is this for them to bear fruits and be bold
The season of colours has stored for us everything in umpteen
Flamboyant's reddish call or hues of last Holi all fall short to intervene

Published in AZAHAR
Revista Poetica No.130 (Spain)

Dark Truth

Fusion of vices with fetid of silent valley,

so much painful, disgusting and suffocating,

Drifting my body, soul and mind

with its infecting substance sorely.

When harvesting crops of fulfillment discerns

the path of myriad opportunities

I stand on the threshold

to become a patriarch again

for bygone causes well known as sorcery.

Look at the upheaval of waves of sordid thoughts contagious,

smearing so quickly me , making me helpless to surrender

before an urge, that blossoms only in nocturnal darkness.

My solicitous soul asks me, quarrels and

I engage in a soliloquy with myself,

the fruits of which are yet to have a name!

The way-out, seems a farthest star still twinkling

The take-home materials, though contending and contrary

I see there circles of smoke,

means ember exists beneath the carpet of ashes,

ignition sneaks from my cozy heart's chamber!

Dark

If you delve into dark

Gather only dark and dark

Sometimes solid,

May be liquid or else

In other times gaseous.

On plain soil, uneven or muddy

Wherever, keeping on which tune, lyric,

Being engrossed

See the dark in open eyes,

If not able to see in eyes

See it in own feelings

By closing eyes.

Dark is round, thin, simple

Of all kinds, all shapes

But not formless, not even aberration.

Dark is the spokesperson of its own,

Only it can detect its existence,

Creation and destruction

With its nail tip or

May not do so.

As dark is soundless, emotionless, edgeless,

empathyless and yielding free

There may not be sign of stigma

In dark or else

Courage to through away the light.

Dark is dark

Which is not absence of the light

Not veil of the night

Not the replica of black even.

Published in Himalaya Diary, 30th March, 2025(Nepal)

Colouring of Self

Spirited and engrossed by seasonal hues myriad
I gossip with towering own self not being tired
In this April when all from top to bottom talk about colours
How their unadulterated veracity to interfere every soul porous
For a beginning untamed by unshakable skills to step forward
As muse of bees resounds like a clarion call from the backyard

The Sun's shinning sprays colours of white seem vibrant
In my mind's canvas paints rising courage sans any rant
Rejoicing with nature and getting applause from within
Whistling away pages of bottlenecks from chapters that intertwine
Dotting the mishaps as the sign of standstill perhaps

Overcoming slowly myself from deep somber flip flops

Applying hues of hope immense in eyes tearful
Self confidence evolves around here and there as tool
That de-escalates agonies as if with melodies of the oud's
And drives away from life's sky constantly mounted dark clouds
The light post is not faraway that tingles in colours superior
Soon w'll emerge as the champion nurturing
traits of a warrior, lone survivor

Published in Himalaya Diary, 30th March, 2025 (Nepal)

Perpetual Game

Among does and don'ts so many
When emotions fly high in sky
Strings of all our efforts numerous
Fail to lift the kite from falling down
There below the sky canopy so vast
Curly attitudes often sneak
Amidst blurred clouds uncertain
Garbage of thoughts in mind blink
Unworthy feelings of the Satan reverberates
Lowering self-esteem fundamentals crucial
In this game of shadow and light
Shadow consumes brightness very often
The ongoing moments display sights trivial
Poor show of righteousness frightens
Vice extends its wings so complex
Values and ethos hide face in shame
Fight for superiority seems incessant
Between virtues, the hero of aspirations recognized
And vice, the villain of denigrations patronized
Virtue curtails vice's wings then as threshold is touched

Honestly crops up as value paramount
Impartiality steps into fasten the grip
Seeking to promote the glory of humanity surpassing evil
Duty is worshipped as the replica of deity
Sans surrendering integrity to insanity
But still then below the nose vice awaits to renew the game
The game of throne continues as before the same.

Published in The Mirror of Time, June, 2023(West Bengal)

Poem

Guess I, poems for me have become faraway stars
navigating the blue sky so vast
Now I fathom them only as my dreams' theme
hidden in bygone past
They twinkle to unfold my creative petals the whole night
Gossip not as silence of profundity may be disturbed in fright
Perhaps reminiscing they mindfully
our days of watertight bonding
Merrymaking, cuddling that unwrap essence of life
deeply grounding
Night as usual approaching eastwards to greet the morning star
But me is in crossfire
beholding the faded beauty of the evening star
Miles to go unnoticed before we can pen a memorabilia
Poems burn me every now and then with sweet nostalgia
Being optimistic is good

that brings new morning infected in glowing sunshine
Presence of the moon in its totality will compel stars
to hide their faces under clouds nine
Don't knock the closed door
as it may have housed the unexpected opportunity profound
Let the tiny seed naturally sprout
sans any manly intervention all around
Cordial relationship is very hard to break,
very much solid and sound
Let not give scope to the time so cruel
tell about the story of the wound
Poems are too delicate,
succinct not them when the mood is wayward
Let the situation
like the tide swells as well as fuels to carry forward
Fragile are not poems,
but changes colour even in sunny days
Patiently hear
how the mind's bird frolicking in humour and says.

Something Indifferent

Now, I am withdrawing myself
like an amphibious tortoise
Want to live within my self-made jurisdiction
but not in disguise
Closing all my physical and metaphysical identities
for a purpose seems to me wise.

Not that it's for sheer self-defense, pacifism indeed
Where one remains aloof for the sake of
extraordinary situations valid
Or else to cover-up own inability like an escapist stupid.

Here the alluring outer world behaves
as a trespasser in my view
At a particular turning point I realized
Self-esteem is sine qua non,
above any sort of self-motivated agenda's purview
Non compromising attitude I welcome,
for overcoming the widespread present day
humiliating statuesque.

Self advertising becomes a curse
when it touches the line forbidden
When interpersonal fellow feelings
encash unjust dividend golden
This aggravating situation
compels swiftly persons like me
to remain in hidden.

Have you seen anywhere?
or else heard the story of the lion lives by eating grass!
Person of worth delineates things apart
not using a colourful sunglass
Not in my opinion it's at any way workable,
for own vested interest to baffle all en masse.

Published in Atunis Galaxy Poetry, 29th March, 2026 (Belgium)

Treasury of Hard Problems

Be it agony of a fallen leaf
Wailing of a burnt valley
Delusion of a plucked bud
Wears all the epithets of a heart broken.
Like a fragmented mirror, a grief stricken splinted heart
modulates only images astronomical.
The shattered self weeps silently,
invisible to eyes naked.
When wisps of unidentified smoke envelopes,
braggadocio suffuses with tints of pewter.
The petrichor of love infected by negligence
embarks upon disabled April wind.
Parallel lines of dysphoria keep bones apart.
North and South Poles don't complement and supplement
like Yin and Yang.
If I continue penning, linking scrap dreams nonstop

You will prefer to fall asleep in billowy surge of ignorance
The oceanic depth of your understanding will be paralyzed
against opprobrium genuine.

Published in Atunis Galaxy Poetry, 29th March, 2026 (Belgium)

N.B: Opprobrium-criticism

Dysphoria- a state of dissatisfaction with life

Braggadocio-arrogant behaviour

Pewter- grey metal

Sometimes

Sometimes to carry the burden of
Seven Dreams on my frozen shoulder
Seems profane, adulterine and guile.
When I start diving across
Seven Layers of Water in succession, procession and obsession
When I start moving above
Seven Clouds of serenity, tranquility and sublimity
Seventh Season bids farewell to me
purposefully, cheerfully and successfully
Being in the state of
unconscious, sub-conscious and consciousness galore !
Nine Emotions of mine scattering
like fallen tube rose petals pristine
Unable completely I to reassemble them for causes
Innumerable, insurmountable and inaccessible sure.

On the way Sat-Chit-Anand mesmerizing me
as dark clouds for the swallow innocent
The Fifth Vedic verses not yet scribbled
I here sometimes rising from my broken self
Bubbling in my mind its endearing rhythm
So vivacious, salacious and marvelous.
The cosmic vibe for me as the believer
Aeonic, iconic and sonic
Entitles me to get respite from
Drowning in the Seven Seas enormous.

N.B:
Published in Atunis Galaxy Poetry, 29th March, 2026 (Belgium)
a. Seven Dreams = far away dreams (Sata Sapana)
b. Seven Layers of Water= Deep water(Sata Tala Pani)
c. Seven Clouds= Dark clouds that bring rain(Sata Megha)
d. Seventh season= Beyond seasonal limitations (Saptama Rutu)
e. Nine emotions= Nine types of emotions like love, anger etc. (Naba Rasa)
f. Fifth Veda= Illusion related(Panchama Beda)
g. Seven seas= amounts to large water bodies (Sata Sagar)

Stigma

I felt stigmatized when you asked my own religion
You may not know faith resides in personal bastion !
I felt victimized when you demanded undue favour
Didn't you know it's unethical to become cynically clever?
Expected I your unquestionable and unrestrained dedication
Labeled you this with societal taboos and dogmas
breeding discrimination
Abandoned you our long cherished dreams quite loveable
Rejected you our alluring feelings very subtle but enjoyable
Stagnation in our reciprocal response put
the ambience under duress
Shattered our wishes here and there
like autumnal falling leaves bearing stress
Bullies drenched me in rains of distrusted returning Monsoon

Carving a niche for our love will not be possible
soon
Disgraceful is your behavior for anyone to bear
On this critical juncture lives of ours proceed out
of gear
Sarcastically I may proclaim now
we move like two parallel lines!
Stigmatization marked an indelible scar
on my forehead which you must opine

Home of Peace

Peace reigns when mind remains calm

Push mind inward to experience it's charm

Paint it's picture on minds hologram

Pray for its stay, let mind to resist jam

Essence of peace is unconditional love

Enter into the zone of peace loving dove

Exaltation of peace empowers it's stake

Everlasting peace rests on forgiveness plank

Arrival of peace needs a tender soft heart

Astounding is it's impact that removes all dirt

Aspiration for peace builds a way for new start

Asylum it provides as all are it's best part

Caring others as own surely enhances
Causation of peace to arrest nuisances

Cosmopolitan outlook removes hindrances

Coming on the way of peace for instances

Euphoria of peace is coated with sympathy

Enter into a stage that permits empathy

Eternal peace ensures our sustainability

Eagerness to promote peace should be our priority

Untitled Bond

Bidding adieu sometimes
may not be the end of a long-standing fray !
It may be adorned with intentions
to transform the area of grey!
You must have known
lovable people are capable to bear weather extreme,
They can exchange goodwill
standing apart on opposite sides of the stream.
Lovelorn souls are very fond of
doing highest sacrifice,
Inflicting sufferings on own self
they bestow blessings in disguise.
Though dwell we under one roof,
differences among us crop up seasonally,
Silly matters, avoidable familiar tussles undoubtedly
provoke us to fight in-between generally.
Now the thread of love is incapable
to stitch cleavages among us,
Conjugal relationship of ours

became scapegoat of ephemeral ego and status.
Uncanny sympathy has acquired
the sanctum sanatorium of empathy abruptly,
Can we reside in the same house?
Speak please honestly!
Gone are those days
when we used to share weal and woe,
When keeping hands on own chest
Jovially we had taken flattering vow;
Not to leave each other's hand
even during cases so grim,
Not to step back without helping the other
to cherish the dream ,
But to walk side by side
and chase ups and downs of wedded life,
But to seek unconditional love
and transcend unutterable strife.
Now I let you free from
so-called prejudiced bondage,
Now you need not be condemned
for any sacrilege.
When trust has scattered
like castle of card,
When thrust on belongingness

battered on the market yard,
No exigency can push us
for an amicable compromise.
I bid you goodbye
that may not be for you a surprise!

Winning

Winning is seldom like," I came, I saw, I conquered",
what once one said
Those who won aspire for more
Those who failed still try to lift the stone further

This is a loveable dream
that keeps us sleepless all along
Some may proceed slowly like a tortoise!
Some may go fast like a rabbit seems unwise!

Sometimes failure brings contentment
to some narcissus souls
This abnormality, sense of negative winning
Helps to cherish one's hedonistic feeling

Ups and downs are two sides of our life
Now who occupied the throne being the king
May be dethroned within seconds of eye lid's twinkling!

After every interval there exists ray of hope
Even at the end of the tunnel there may be light!
Winners are capable to surpass even any weird fright

Winners possess fire in belly intrinsically
Hard work always pay is for them pious line of the gospel
Herald they new dawn when darkness seems hard to dispel

Black

Observed I the black day
when you broke my trust
Since then emotionally I am in coma,
unable to meet your lust
Your black magic on me
yielded desired results galore
A black sheep I became
although was famous for my valour
Cunningly you played the role
to put me in black books
Unfortunately I lost everything even
the lifting attitudinal hooks
Now I am internally bankrupt
as you resorted to blackmail
I become a blackhead
on the face of the societal trail
Believe me, I am not in a position
to face your black look
Vagabond I became, you made me a pauper
by hook or by crock
Your deeds are scribed in black and white
on my mind's canvas

You caused my black listing
when I was trying to escape through virtuous underpass
You will certainly earn the name of black spot
all times to come
Now I enjoy black comedy for relaxation
without minding the outcome

Is Peace an Illusion?

Sometimes a pertinent question is raised;
Why after all in this world peace is to be praised?
When everywhere we see peace is murdered,
In broad daylight, before everyone, it's maimed.
Look at our history of great human
race 's intention,
It's characterized with violence, mayhem and tension.
At the same time always there
the need of peace was retained,
At every interval a room for peace was maintained.
This is the game of hide and seek for peace's arrival,
This is the backup on which depends our survival.
Our very existence is for peace, bliss and contentment;
On these bases stand our society?
its progress and future prospect.
Peace is real, not an illusion, not a misnomer,
Only with peace we cherish our dreams and prosper.

Cosmopolitan outlook, its expansion
to every nook and corner of the world as such,
How difficult it may be, brings coordination, cooperation
for lasting peace very much!
We are humans first and this is our all time explanation,
Race, religion, region like tags are illusory justification.
Only by dint of love, tolerance, fellowship and brotherhood,
Peace like heavenly attribute can only be ensured for good.
War begets war, violence begets violence,
Peace begets peace; it's the tool of cosmic adherence.

Katakan Riot

When toxins of suspicion, intolerance, jealousy and disbelief
Moved to the core
The thread of relationship
Like the cut off kite having been losing the direction
Moves haphazardly, here and there.
Falls down on the earth or on the electricity poll,
sticking to the tree boughs
Reminiscing once the bygone times.

With the cool touch of time
Wounds recuperate gently.
With the advancement of the day
From the canvas of mind
An worrisome dream bids farewell
Not to approach again, not at all.

Whether the foot prints of Prophet Muhammad
or the foot prints of Sri Chaitanya
Beholding the feet, loud call emerges in the mind.
Soil, water and wind's union
With devotional offerings becomes one and all

To harvest modest delightfulness in the desert of life.

Town of fifty two marts and pathways of fifty three
With a few pennies amassed by Baimundi
Laying the foundation stone of
flood restrained embankment
From Gadgadia Ghat to Debigada
Our Kataka is appealing and humorous.

Just now a black cloud of kingship
Flouts in the firmament of Kataka
To pour open big -budget opulence of
Affection, love, care and intimacy.
Just now in this millennium city
Notwithstanding the last tears of fury and frustration
The eternal alliance is branching out.

From Matamatha to Manisahu,very crowded square
Too much rush of people,
Within the harsh sounds of vehicles
The existence of Kataka seems unique.

Therefore staying hydra headed thrilling
Since some days occupied the place
The song of daily chores
Of everyday living of Katakans.

Buxi Bazar, the birth place of Netaji, Odia Bazar, Kadam Rasul and City Hospital, the square of Durgha Bazar
Everywhere Kataka in her own toilette
Sometimes is in work, sometimes is perturbed,
Sometimes feels suffocation,
Sometimes displays her competence through Dahibara making.

Let Kataka to bloom in her own terms and conditions
To gather millions of silver filigree dreams,

To swim together in the rough waters either at Naraj or at Jobra.
Let Katakans to pick from the banks of river Kathjodi
A handful of drowsy endearment
To embellish the braid of Katakianis.
Let's come together to immerse
In the swift streams of Mahanadi
Heaps of stale flowers resembling with brawls.

Listening to the Azaan
While arranging the watch hands
Let's wander in Hatipokhari
Where it is said
Once throwing one Palmyra palm fruit of malice
One crow flew away for good.

Baripada is Well

You don't know perhaps!
Not everything has altered
During these three decades long stretching of time.
Even now pulling the veil of cloud
Moon of 'Radhakrushna Bhanja"
Keeps its dazzling chalky face hidden.
When the lights of the town switch off
Chatting Box and wakeful eyebrows of the sweetheart combust.
Bearing not pitiless thrashing of time
Your long and waist touching braid
Though becoming shrink!
But now here Baripada long ago
Taking a lengthy sigh
After winding up a sweeping jump to Palbani.
Like in the past when dusk wraps 'Swagatika'
Aroma of Mahua imbues throughout.
When rain fashions honeymoon in Similipal
Who will become the heroine of the partridge?
Becomes the subject of debate in Baripada.
From that day yours' kohl scribbled
Black and white rough tale pail

On the chest of Baripada, Bhanjabhumi
Appears as greenish as folioles of Sal tree.
Whose long, pressed chuckle
Audible from the chamber of Bishram Lodge!
Mild gossip but heighten panting!
Like before lackluster post office
Dispenses service increasingly.
Seems you are there,
There rests your virgin mind bathing place steps.
No one sees movie of 'Bijoy Mohanty '!
No movie, no rush
You are not, am not
Many sensations of past still remain
amidst unscratched nope.
Equal footing with the high speed of night time bus
Boils the body in boundless heat.
Generates in mind killer waves,
Dimness fabricates illimitable fright.
'Garamagaram' and 'Mohapatra Hotel'
On the go in trading,
Taste buds emanate in tongue, luscious.
Picturesque, fabulous Baripada 's greatness
Unfeasible to be dismantled with,

'Ambika' has kept its pristine under the veil of her saree.

Yes, Baripada is well
Just like you.
On her voluptuous body depicted
An overflowing unbridled river.
Transposed geography only,
Ever growing body posture
Calling you waving hands,
Being fond of the back of time
To offer here
Once again gifts of love.

My living, not of Satan

Am in dilemma
Of indecisiveness,
The fruit of which
Bears no seeds at all.
If I befriend with
The side of rapture,
Lights blink to remind
That sorrow's shadow
Ensures my existence.
When I handshake with
Stark reality of agony
Darkness indulges in gossip.
Let's arrive at a solution
And invoke co-existence.
Where the wind
That blows eastwards
Engulf surely in plentitude
The fragrance of wind
That travels to westward.
The overflowing river
That inundates habitats
Keeps the promise
To bring back greenery.

These prelude the abyss
Of my being as human
And include the terrace
Of my living, not of Satan.

Being Naked

Being naked I want to roam free like the Jain saints
All virgin places undiscovered before, not colonized
Habitats faraway from mainland's hustle and bustle
Sea beaches not even smoked by tourists in profound
Thick jungles full with wild beasts,
poisonous snakes and birds of many hues
But not exploited by human greed and double edged gesture
I want to navigate being naked sans having any roars
Off boarding at any islet that still cherishes
the glory of nature bountiful
Climb high rising mountain peaks dazzling with contentment
Where even human's shadow failed to signature its presence
Really I want to be forgotten, to remain in isolation

For a cause, a purpose, a valid mission
better to be kept enveloped
Rather than making disclosure
for the outer business bound exploitative world
As I know being naked makes me
shielded against the earthly chorus
So vicious, vociferous that like a volcano
shallows me only when
I am not naked, looks presented
as if like mannequin in attires of thousands desires
,
All artificial, affordable for people in power,
rich and lavishing by stature.

The Other World

The soloist sings song to dethrone ideas of life,
Still then life doesn't evaporate!
Rather gathers from dust vapour to unmask the hypocrisy,
This silent tussle stretches its wings, envelops the whole cosmos.
And endurance being a humane solvent adds uncanny choices,
When neighborhood cliffs are very hard and adventures.
What one gets, when enjoyable events are saturated
with blasphemous ignorance?
Our very existence in this world if disables reciprocity,
We will be unsociable parasites of the other world.
The tit bit of living in harmony,
After being blurred will lost its symphony in wilderness!
Is not it possible, by shedding selfish from self
Self-will itself sing song in chorus,
Enchanting the self, selfhood and the porous divider!

Smokey, The Dog

I know you echo within us
Our vigilant eyes surrenders to your vivid cunningness
Your living and livelihood centers round
Not beyond the very periphery of our house
Your day begins and night ends
Encircling our family chores and morbid notes
You inspect every movement, every nitty gritty with care
What happens, why happens and how
Interferes you in everything, keeping an eye
In our ups and downs like relationship gamut
you notice everything being the epicenter
In our gossip you participate without any utterances
By your unique behaviour we know your appetite, mood to move in the outside
You calculate our ascending order and descending
For engraving in the history
From your eyes, your body language one knows the unknown

You justify your rights in everything, in any omits and commits
You stand always on the front being the protector
Tongue of yours always seeks the unforeseen,
licking shows signs of belonging,
saliva gathers amongst dust love and affection
Your raised ears are adept to hear even pin drops
Your tail tells stories of togetherness in its every swaying
Overlooking broad intimacy how can we estrange you from ourselves
Our inner self murmurs eventually to lay both hands
On your silky furs, though black in colour
But bright in loveable gesture
Sans an iota of we-ness is it possible to be mad in longings
Feelings of one-ness overshadows certainly distorted selfishness
Faithfulness in galore you reap being true to the soil and camaraderie

Daughter

Sans effluents of lust and leer

Dipping in love and longing

I recall moments though tiny

Filled with emotions enormous

When you started creeping

Encircled my universe's wholeness in toto.

Now at this umpteenth juncture

So melodious and mellifluous

When you are sculpturing

Being the cause of a new universe

Self-made and self-feed

Decor in secured water tightness

My thoughts fly above the nightmare.

My astounding counts of many

Unforeseen mishaps, ill conceived

In bizarre narratives unfounded

Nowhere, in no precincts

Faded away into the abyss of

Misfortune drawn ghettos.

Pleasantries wrapped in passions

Percolating slowly with rhythm

Everywhere like morning dews

Dazzling as gold precious

And I, the lone traveler, submersing in ecstasy of fulfilling

Starting to name the stars that twinkling.

Love and Lust

When lust overpowers love
Servitude remains in fray
To hankering women, flesh in all.
A slight difference, like a tiny thread
Exists between them.
Sometimes it is visible,
In other times wraps
In blurred values
Undistinguishable, unfathomable.
Emotional eruption
When rides the ladder
Perfumes of exotica
Favours the most
Notwithstanding the inner call
So judicious but seems
Vague and voluminous.
Alluvial deposits benefit
So also love, affection and belonging.
When obsession reigns over
From all fronts instantly
Decency churns into pieces
And like a broken mirror

It reflects showcasing
Instinct of an animal.
Love between a child and mother
And love at the old age
Amongst a loving couple
Preserves love in its
Pure form, transparent, very soothing,
Free from malice and taints.
Conjugal loyalty very often
Fails the test of love
So simple but in ample
That possess magical prowess
To overcome rough terrain
That it habitually browses.

Guinea Pig

Treating me lightly

Like a fallen leaf

At the threshold of whirlpool

And encashing on my

Humble backups unheard

Utilizing the porous border

That I admire honestly

To be my best companion

Exists to explore and examine

The blowing facts and figures,

You and your trusted comrades

In broad daylight

Initiated steps in profound disguise

To carry out trials in me

On new things, new proposals

Just agreed upon circulars many,

As I am the guinea pig

Born and brought up clandestinely

To laid my evangelical shoulder

For others to climb the ladder

Of success, triumphs

To immolate my life

For others' well-being

Opt for green pasture to survive

And I the midnight child

Of the stubborn time

Lives only to witness the happenings

Accrue testimony valuable

That's profitable and promising

But not of mine.

Axing Own Self

It's not mere fatality of any type
Not the ambiguous fate that exhibits cruelty
Not the act of any celestial entity ethereal
Believe me, it's the self-earned dividend of other kind
Purely the case of anthropogenic factor very stunning!
When one forgets societal needs and wraps everything
Under the veil of self-aggrandizement, selfishness and arrogance
The net result is sure to be in descending order!
At the outset one may tune the strings of the guitar
To cherish own self, to flourish parochial intentions
Every time, before everyone one may pretend to be the victim
One may relish the act of shoot out
Keeping gun on the shoulder of others
Assuming own self the iconic example of victimization

Very versatile one may be in handling the blame game
Wearing a coloured glass of own choice
One may roam here and there, everywhere to showcase
One's views and propagate news of propaganda hydra headed!
But as time flies with its wings unnoticeable
One will definitely understand a little bit but still then
may presume as well to be the boss!
This process has no end show to celebrate the happy ending
Or else arrangement of a morning session of no use
Its starting point and the end note are blurred in nowhere!
Nothing will happen till the self is liberated,
Conditioned to bloom for spreading fragrance for one and all
Non the less this vicious circle of stubborn reality
Will only change its colors to suit the vested interest astronomical!

Gutter of my Being

Rhythmically random thoughts of my mind when extends
To envelop the vast canvas of bygone days both sweet and sour,
Tear drops accumulate on the corner of the eyes.
Slightly visible smile emanates from lip's distance horizon
And firecracker like light and sound perform somewhere,
Musical notes of an old song pulsate in the backyard.
Thoughts swim in the sea of my mind perturbed,
Drowning may bring havoc as thoughts are cherished but not retailed.
When tides inside me denied overflowing the banks,
I was then extinguishing my own immaculate desire
Using hands soiled by something not discernible.
Welcoming the realisation that me not the heir of that time,

Should I sleep inside the gutter of my being?
Where reigns only glimpses of non-provocation

Adorned with nothingness of a past event, seems blurred.

music

the music of life reinforces rhythm of weal and woes,
hues of longings engulf the whole spectrum titbits
or trailing tentacles of vapour simmers down the innocence offbeat .
chaos mutilates in life's summer
or ecstasy celebrates in life' spring,
but life surpasses both the abyss of horror and the valley of fortune lot.
not to be collided with or even part with the passing time
that changes bed sans any intervals,
but indulges in life's pure mathematics
so frightened and cumbersome to grasp,
digest and weave tactics.
but gossiping of life in the form of paranoid rhyme
still seems earmarking a place
where life generates celestial music extravaganza
and as crystal as autumnal sky
that besets unique poetic stanza

ABOUT THE POET

Dr. Alok Kumar Ray is a well-known litterateur in the arena of both Odia and English language, literature and culture. As the epitome of an erudite scholar, Political Science textbooks authored by him are being taught in higher secondary and graduate levels in both Odisha and the North-Eastern states of our country. Many of his research based articles on literature, culture, socio-economic themes, current affairs and poems have been featured in various magazines, newspapers, anthologies, websites etc. across the globe and have obtained wide applause due to readership ratings. He has two monolingual, one each bilingual and multilingual poetry collections named as Meghapanata, Sillage, Trouvaille and Kalijahna respectively. In addition Dr. Ray is a former member of international voluntary organizations i.e. **Red Cross and Rotary International.**

Dr. Ray's collection of poems named as 'Badhuli' (Balsams) is a poetic expression of eternal thoughts and habitual but cross cultural overtones like life and livelihood, love and passion, both earthly and heavenly joys and sorrows. In it, eyes resembling the ocean dream, while embracing the beach. But when lips, reminiscing about the salty taste afterwards, sometimes blame the night and itself in other times while recapitulating and at the very eve, the morning star blinks its eyes residing in mind's sky. The irrefutable possibility of living as a woman rather than being born a woman, which has to be proven every moment, its verbal explosion when looms over 'Badhuli' , societal constraints like the high rising waves of the ocean challenge it and make it insatiable every time. Most of the poems accommodated in 'Badhuli' persist, taking refuge in such a fragile base. In it, the reader will internalize the blessings of being a girl or a woman less and more often as the curse in his cozy heart, and will try to delineate picture of his likeness in his mind's canvas. If Badhuli can achieve this, then it will consider itself blessed. Then, lying on the lap of the earth under the open sky, using collegium, 'Badhuli' will see sometimes as it has shaped the clouds like demons by own creative efforts, sometimes like mountains, birds, humans and Gods, but has not given them any form that is blurred and incomprehensible, that will be judged in terms of mechanical stereotypes, and then only it will amass self-actualization.

Indian Writing in English